# OREMUS

## A GUIDE TO CATHOLIC PRAYER

## STUDENT WORKBOOK

Fr. Mark Toups

ASCENSION PRESS

West Chester, Pennsylvania

*Nihil obstat:*    Rev. Matthew J. Gutowski, S.T.L.
                  *Censor Librorum*
                  January 27, 2013

*Imprimatur:*    +Most Reverend George J. Lucas
                  Archbishop of Omaha
                  January 27, 2013

*Oremus* is an adult faith formation resource of Ascension Press.

Excerpts from the English translation of the *Catechism of the Catholic Church* for use in the United States of America. Copyright © 1994, 1997, United States Catholic Conference, Inc.–Libreria Editrice Vaticana. All rights reserved.

Unless otherwise noted, Scripture passages have been taken from the *Revised Standard Version–Catholic Edition.* © Copyright 1946, 1952, 1971 by the Division of Christian Education of the National Council of the Churches of Christ in the United States of America. All rights reserved.

Scripture passages marked "NAB" are from the *New American Bible.* Copyright © 1987, by World Bible Publishers, Inc. All rights reserved.

This book contains selected excerpts from *The Discernment of Spirits: An Ignatian Guide for Everyday Living,* by Father Timothy Gallagher. Published by The Crossroad Publishing Company, 2005. Reprinted with permission of the publisher (crossroadpublishing.com).

Ascension Press
Post Office Box 1990
West Chester, PA 19380
Customer service: 1-800-376-0520
AscensionPress.com

Cover design: Devin Schadt

Printed in the United States of America

ISBN: 978-1-935940-46-3

# CONTENTS

# A Letter from Fr. Mark Toups

**Welcome to *Oremus*!\*** Over the next eight weeks, you are going to be inspired to deepen your prayer life while learning how to open yourself to God and receive everything he wants for you in prayer. As Catholics, we have a deep spiritual heritage in classic forms of prayer, including meditation, contemplation, and the spiritual senses. These rich forms of Christian prayer allow us to "dive deep" into the oceans of God's merciful love.

In her autobiography, St. Thèrése of Lisieux describes prayer in this way: "For me, prayer is a surge of the heart; it is a simple look turned toward heaven; it is a cry of recognition and of love, embracing both trial and joy"[4] (CCC 2558). If you're hungry for this "surge of the heart," this study is for *you*.

**Would you like to hear God speak to you?** When many Catholics hear the words "meditation" and "contemplative prayer," their eyes glaze over and their thoughts wander. Such practices, they think, are reserved to priests, monks, and nuns; lay people certainly cannot do such things. Yet God calls all Christians, regardless of their state in life, to grow in holiness; this type of prayer provides the means to a deepened relationship with the Lord. However, all of us—including you—are invited to grow in an intimate relationship with God through the gift of prayer.

*Oremus* will provide you with the basics on both meditative and contemplative prayer, concentrating in a special way on a form of praying with the Bible known as *lectio divina*, as well as on "imaginative" prayer, a way of praying that allows the Holy Spirit to guide your spiritual senses. The principles of this study are drawn from the *Spiritual Exercises* of Saint Ignatius of Loyola.

**About the *Oremus* program.** There are eight sessions in the *Oremus* program. At each session, I will guide you through an easy-to-understand teaching on prayer. After each presentation, you will engage in a small-group discussion of the truths you just heard. You will also have a chance to talk about any challenges or developments you wish to share with the group from the previous week.

Here's the best part: In between sessions, you will be invited to pray using specific Scripture passages in your workbook. I'll give you a Scripture passage every day for the eight weeks. It's like making an eight-week retreat in the midst of your busy life! You will also be invited to keep track of your thoughts and progress through short journal entries that you will be making in your workbook. These weeks are designed to help guide you step-by-step to draw close to God and to listen for his voice speaking to you.

I'm looking forward to walking with you. See you soon at *Oremus*!

In Christ,

*Fr. Mark Toups*

Fr. Mark Toups

---

\**Oremus* \ō-'rā-müs\ is a Latin word meaning "Let us pray."

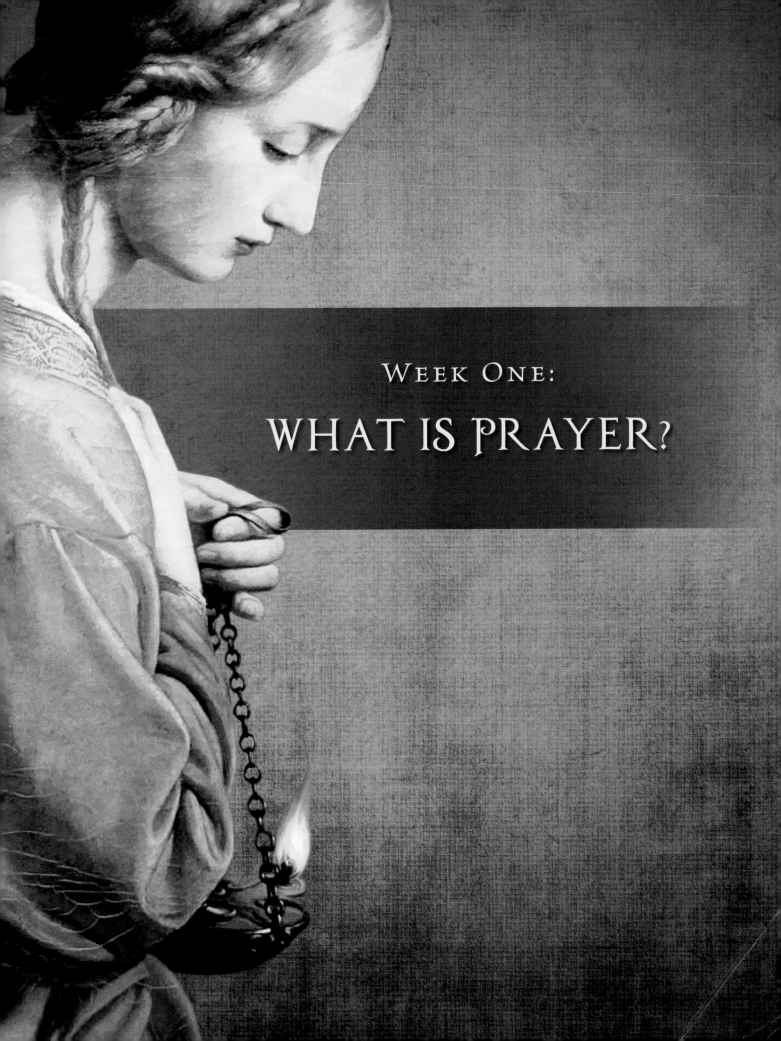

WEEK ONE:

# WHAT IS PRAYER?

# What Is Prayer?
# SESSION OUTLINE

1. *"Man is in search of God.* In the act of creation, God calls every being from nothingness into existence. ... Even after losing through his sin his likeness to God, man remains an image of his Creator, and retains the desire for the one who calls him into existence. All religions bear witness to men's essential search for God." –CCC 2566[1]

2. "Human life without prayer, which opens our existence to the mystery God, lacks sense and direction." –Pope Benedict XVI[2]

3. "Many Christians are aware of the necessity and the beauty of contemplative prayer and have a sincere yearning for it. Yet, apart from tentative efforts soon abandoned, few remain faithful to this mode of prayer, and even fewer are really convinced and satisfied by their own practice of it. ... We would like to pray, but we cannot manage it. ... Our time of prayer passes, leaving us distracted, and since it does not seem to yield any tangible fruit, we are not loath to give up. From time to time we take up a book of 'meditations,' which presents us, ready-made, with the contemplation we ought to produce for ourselves. ... Often ... fearfulness ... robs us of the confidence to take steps on our own." –Hans Urs von Balthazar[3]

4. "He was praying in a certain place, and when he ceased, one of his disciples said to him, 'Lord, teach us to pray, as John taught his disciples.'" –Luke 11:1

5. "It is in fact in Jesus that man becomes able to approach God in the depth and intimacy of the relationship of fatherhood and sonship. Together with the first disciples, let us now turn with humble trust to the Teacher and ask him: 'Lord, teach us to pray.'" –Pope Benedict XVI[4]

6. "God calls man first. Man may forget his Creator or hide far from his face; he may run after idols or accuse the deity of having abandoned him; yet the living and true God tirelessly calls each person to that mysterious encounter known as prayer. In prayer ... God's initiative of love always comes first; our own first step is always a response." –CCC 2567

7. "It was not you who chose me but I who chose you." –John 15:16, NAB

8. "A step or two before the place where I am to contemplate or meditate, I will stand for the space of an Our Father and, with my consciousness raised on high, consider how the Lord my God looks upon me. Then I will make an act of reverence or humility." –St. Ignatius of Loyola[5]

9. "*We have come to believe in God's love*: in these words the Christian can express the fundamental decision of his life. Being Christian is not the result of an ethical choice or a lofty idea, but the encounter with an event, a person, which gives life a new horizon and a decisive direction." –Pope Benedict XVI[6]

10. "We receive the first lesson from the Lord by his example. The Gospels describe Jesus to us in intimate and constant conversation with the Father: it is a profound communion of the One who came into the world not to do his will but that of the Father who sent him for the salvation of man." –Pope Benedict XVI[7]

11. "Yet only in God who reveals himself does man's seeking find complete fulfillment. The prayer that is openness and elevation of the heart to God, thus becomes a personal relationship with him. And even if man forgets his Creator, the living, true God does not cease to call man first to the mysterious encounter of prayer." –Pope Benedict XVI[8]

12. "For I know well the plans I have in mind for you, says the Lord, plans for your welfare, not for woe! plans to give you a future full of hope. When you call me, when you go to pray to me, I will listen to you. When you look for me, you will find me. Yes, when you seek me with all your heart, you will find me with you, says the Lord." –Jeremiah 29:11-14, NAB

# DISCUSSION

### QUESTION #1

What challenges do you face in your prayer life? Explain.

### QUESTION #2

Describe your experience of prayer before hearing this week's teaching.

### QUESTION #3

What stayed with you the most from the teaching this week?

### QUESTION #4

What do you desire most from God as you begin this eight-week study?

### QUESTION #5

What do you desire most from God during your prayer time?

# DAY 1

WEEK #1

FOR YOUR PRAYER

# JEREMIAH 29:11-14

Read the passage once to become familiar with the text.

Slowly read the passage a second time.

Very, very slowly read the passage a third time.

Pay attention to which word, words, or phrases captures your attention or tugs at your heart.

Talk to God about what is on your heart … and listen.

### JOURNAL

*The "strongest" thought or feeling during my prayer was …*

when I relized that God was there for me,
wating for me to talk to him.

*My heart "rested" when …*

I found peace in my heart
while praying.

*I sense the Lord was telling me …*

I need to truest him more.
have more faith in him.

*I ended the prayer wanting …*

I wanted to be more at piece while praying
and not to be so distracted while praying.
asking God to help me to listen to what,
he was saying to me.

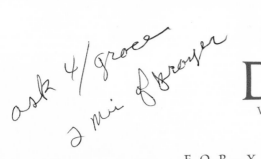
*ask 4/ grace*
*7 min of prayer*

# DAY 2
WEEK #1

FOR YOUR PRAYER

# JOHN 15:1-17

Read the passage once to become familiar with the text.

Slowly read the passage a second time.

Very, very slowly read the passage a third time.

Pay attention to which word, words, or phrases captures your attention or tugs at your heart.

Talk to God about what is on your heart … and listen.

### JOURNAL

*The "strongest" thought or feeling during my prayer was …*

praying for the people and especially the little children who in the war zones. I felt that God was telling me to trust in him.

*My heart "rested" when …*

I felt that God was there listening to my concerns.

*I sense the Lord was telling me …*

to remain in him and he will remain in me.

*I ended the prayer wanting …*

to do more in prayer for others —

# DAY 3
### WEEK #1

## FOR YOUR PRAYER

# PSALMS 139:1-18

Read the passage once to become familiar with the text.

Slowly read the passage a second time.

Very, very slowly read the passage a third time.

Pay attention to which word, words, or phrases captures your attention or tugs at your heart.

Talk to God about what is on your heart ... and listen.

### JOURNAL

*The "strongest" thought or feeling during my prayer was ...*

I felt I was not alone in prayer.
I felt that I was really talking to God

*My heart "rested" when ...*

I finish my prayer, I felt I had told God
what was in my heart

*I sense the Lord was telling me ...*

that he knew I was very concern about
what I was praying for, and not to worry
because he was taking care of things

*I ended the prayer wanting ...*

to be closer to God.

# DAY 4
WEEK #1

FOR YOUR PRAYER

# ROMANS 8:22-27

Read the passage once to become familiar with the text.

Slowly read the passage a second time.

Very, very slowly read the passage a third time.

Pay attention to which word, words, or phrases captures your attention or tugs at your heart.

Talk to God about what is on your heart … and listen.

JOURNAL

*The "strongest" thought or feeling during my prayer was …*

that the Holy spirit was there to intercede
for us in our weaknesses.

*My heart "rested" when …*

I felt what a blessing we have to
know we can come to God.

*I sense the Lord was telling me …*

that I need to be more confident, have
more trust in my prayers to him.

*I ended the prayer wanting …*

to be more deeper in my prayers to God

# DAY 5
### WEEK #1

## FOR YOUR PRAYER

# ROMANS 8:31-39

Read the passage once to become familiar with the text.

Slowly read the passage a second time.

Very, very slowly read the passage a third time.

Pay attention to which word, words, or phrases captures your attention or tugs at your heart.

Talk to God about what is on your heart … and listen.

### JOURNAL

*The "strongest" thought or feeling during my prayer was …*

that God was ready to hear my prayer – It made me feel at peace

*My heart "rested" when …*

When I felt I was saying the right words for my prayer.

*I sense the Lord was telling me …*

that nothing could come between God, me and my prayers.

*I ended the prayer wanting …*

I wanted to keep thanking God for the blessings I have received thru out my life.

# DAY 6
### WEEK #1

FOR YOUR PRAYER

# PSALM 63

Read the passage once to become familiar with the text.

Slowly read the passage a second time.

Very, very slowly read the passage a third time.

Pay attention to which word, words, or phrases captures your attention or tugs at your heart.

Talk to God about what is on your heart … and listen.

### JOURNAL

*The "strongest" thought or feeling during my prayer was …*

how much I look for God in my daily
needs of my life

*My heart "rested" when …*

when I felt I am probably not alone
when I look for God in prayer —
when I feel so helpless;
I am always look for God in prayer.

*I sense the Lord was telling me …*

to talk to him anytime.

*I ended the prayer wanting …*

Wanting to be more deeply in the
presence of God.

*Romans*
*8-31-39*

# DAY 7
### WEEK #1

## FOR YOUR PRAYER

Return to the Scripture passage that spoke to you the most this week.

Read the passage once to become familiar with the text.

Slowly read the passage a second time.

Very, very slowly read the passage a third time.

Pay attention to which word, words, or phrases captures your attention or tugs at your heart.

Talk to God about what is on your heart … and listen.

### JOURNAL

*The "strongest" thought or feeling during my prayer was …*

_____
_____
_____
_____

*My heart "rested" when …*

_____
_____
_____
_____

*I sense the Lord was telling me …*

_____
_____
_____
_____

*I ended the prayer wanting …*

_____
_____
_____
_____

Week Two:

# BEFORE YOU PRAY

# Before You Pray
# SESSION OUTLINE

## Step One – Find the right time.

1. "Each one of us needs time and space for recollection, meditation, and calmness. ... Thanks be to God that this is so! In fact, this need tells us that we are not made for work alone, but also to think, to reflect or even simply to follow with our minds and our hearts a tale, a story in which to immerse ourselves, in a certain sense 'to lose ourselves' to find ourselves subsequently enriched." –Pope Benedict XVI[1]

2. "Making time for God regularly is a fundamental element for spiritual growth; it will be the Lord himself who gives us the taste for his mysteries, his words, his presence and action, for feeling how beautiful it is when God speaks with us; he will enable us to understand more deeply what he expects of me." –Pope Benedict XVI[2]

3. A few important questions about you:

   • When are you most receptive?

   • When are you most uninterrupted?

   • What time is most consistently open?

4. A few important questions about your commitments to other people:

   • What commitments have you made to your spouse?

   • What commitments have you made to your family?

   • What commitments have you made to others, such as to your job or school?

   **Consider:** *Might any of these commitments need to be sacrificed or re-prioritized in order to meet your commitments to God?*

5. There's a difference between recreation and re-creation:

  • Start slow

  • Be realistic

  • Be consistent

  • Grow gradually

## Step Two – Select a Scripture passage ahead of time.

6. "Through his Word, God speaks to man." –CCC 2700

7. How do you find a Scripture passage?

  • Readings for daily Mass

  • Readings for the upcoming Sunday

  • Slowly read through the Gospels: Mark, Matthew, Luke, John

  • Slowly read through the Psalms

## Step Three – Pay attention to your desires.

8. "Saint Augustine, in a homily on the *First Letter of John*, describes very beautifully the intimate relationship between prayer and hope. He defines prayer as an exercise of desire." –Pope Benedict XVI[3]

9. "And if the object of one's desire is a relationship with God, his blessing and love, then the struggle cannot fail but ends in that self-giving to God, in recognition of one's own weakness, which is overcome only by giving oneself over into God's merciful hands." –Pope Benedict XVI[4]

10. "We would not be able to pray were the desire for God, for being children of God, not engraved in the depths of our heart." –Pope Benedict XVI[5]

11. "I will ask my Lord for what I want and desire." –St. Ignatius of Loyola[6]

# DISCUSSION

QUESTION #1

How would you describe your experience of prayer this past week?

QUESTION #2

What did you find most interesting from this week's teaching?

QUESTION #3

What is the best time for you to pray?
What challenges do you face with being consistent with this time?

QUESTION #4

How would you describe your overall experience of praying with Scripture?
Is it easy? Is it difficult? Explain.

QUESTION #5

How important are your desires to your prayer? Do you share them with God?
Do you tend to ignore them? Do you feel they are important?

# DAY 1
WEEK # 2

# MATTHEW 11:28-30

Read the passage once to become familiar with the text.

Slowly read the passage a second time.

Very, very slowly read the passage a third time.

Pay attention to which word, words, or phrases captures your attention or tugs at your heart.

Talk to God about what is on your heart ... and listen.

### J O U R N A L

*The "strongest" thought or feeling during my prayer was ...*

_____

_____

_____

_____

*My heart "rested" when ...*

_____

_____

_____

_____

*I sense the Lord was telling me ...*

_____

_____

_____

_____

*I ended the prayer wanting ...*

_____

_____

_____

_____

# DAY 2
#### WEEK #2

## FOR YOUR PRAYER

# ISAIAH 55

Read the passage once to become familiar with the text.

Slowly read the passage a second time.

Very, very slowly read the passage a third time.

Pay attention to which word, words, or phrases captures your attention or tugs at your heart.

Talk to God about what is on your heart ... and listen.

### JOURNAL

*The "strongest" thought or feeling during my prayer was ...*

_____

_____

_____

*My heart "rested" when ...*

_____

_____

_____

*I sense the Lord was telling me ...*

_____

_____

_____

*I ended the prayer wanting ...*

_____

_____

_____

# DAY 3
### WEEK # 2

FOR YOUR PRAYER

# ISAIAH 43:1-7

Read the passage once to become familiar with the text.

Slowly read the passage a second time.

Very, very slowly read the passage a third time.

Pay attention to which word, words, or phrases captures your attention or tugs at your heart.

Talk to God about what is on your heart … and listen.

JOURNAL

*The "strongest" thought or feeling during my prayer was …*

_____

_____

_____

_____

*My heart "rested" when …*

_____

_____

_____

_____

*I sense the Lord was telling me …*

_____

_____

_____

_____

*I ended the prayer wanting …*

_____

_____

_____

# DAY 4
WEEK #2

FOR YOUR PRAYER

# MARK 10:46-52

Read the passage once to become familiar with the text.

Slowly read the passage a second time.

Very, very slowly read the passage a third time.

Pay attention to which word, words, or phrases captures your attention or tugs at your heart.

Talk to God about what is on your heart ... and listen.

JOURNAL

*The "strongest" thought or feeling during my prayer was ...*

_____
_____
_____
_____

*My heart "rested" when ...*

_____
_____
_____
_____

*I sense the Lord was telling me ...*

_____
_____
_____
_____

*I ended the prayer wanting ...*

_____
_____
_____
_____

# DAY 5

WEEK # 2

FOR YOUR PRAYER

# ISAIAH 26:8-13

Read the passage once to become familiar with the text.

Slowly read the passage a second time.

Very, very slowly read the passage a third time.

Pay attention to which word, words, or phrases captures your attention or tugs at your heart.

Talk to God about what is on your heart … and listen.

JOURNAL

*The "strongest" thought or feeling during my prayer was …*

_____

_____

_____

*My heart "rested" when …*

_____

_____

_____

*I sense the Lord was telling me …*

_____

_____

_____

*I ended the prayer wanting …*

_____

_____

_____

# DAY 6
WEEK # 2

# MATTHEW 18:12-14

Read the passage once to become familiar with the text.

Slowly read the passage a second time.

Very, very slowly read the passage a third time.

Pay attention to which word, words, or phrases captures your attention or tugs at your heart.

Talk to God about what is on your heart … and listen.

### JOURNAL

*The "strongest" thought or feeling during my prayer was …*

_____

_____

_____

*My heart "rested" when …*

_____

_____

_____

*I sense the Lord was telling me …*

_____

_____

_____

_____

*I ended the prayer wanting …*

_____

_____

_____

# DAY 7

WEEK #2

FOR YOUR PRAYER

Return to the Scripture passage that spoke to you the most this week.

Read the passage once to become familiar with the text.

Slowly read the passage a second time.

Very, very slowly read the passage a third time.

Pay attention to which word, words, or phrases captures your attention or tugs at your heart.

Talk to God about what is on your heart … and listen.

JOURNAL

*The "strongest" thought or feeling during my prayer was …*

_____
_____
_____
_____

*My heart "rested" when …*

_____
_____
_____
_____

*I sense the Lord was telling me …*

_____
_____
_____
_____

*I ended the prayer wanting …*

_____
_____
_____
_____

Week Three:

*LECTIO DIVINA*

## *Lectio Divina*
# SESSION OUTLINE

"I would like in particular to recall and recommend the ancient tradition of *lectio divina*: the diligent reading of Sacred Scripture accompanied by prayer brings about that intimate dialogue in which the person reading hears God who is speaking, and in praying, responds to him with trusting openness of heart. If it is effectively promoted, this practice will bring to the Church—I am convinced of it—a new spiritual springtime." –Pope Benedict XVI[1]

## *Lectio Divina*

*Lectio divina* (sometimes known simply as *"lectio"*) is Latin for "divine reading."

### Step One: *Lectio*

- Start with a passage from Scripture and become familiar with the text.

- Slowly read the passage a second time.

- Very, very slowly read the passage a third time.

- Pay attention to which word, words, or phrases rest in your heart.

### Step Two: *Meditatio*

- Think about the significant text … what is God saying to you?

- What are the implications of the text in your life?

- "To meditate on what we read helps us to make it our own by confronting it with ourselves. Here, another book is opened: the book of life. … To the extent that we are humble and faithful, we discover in meditation the movements that stir the heart and we are able to discern them." –CCC 2706

## Step Three: *Oratio*

- Talk to God … talk with God … about everything.

- "What is contemplative prayer? St. Teresa answers: 'Contemplative prayer *[oracion mental]* in my opinion is nothing else than a close sharing between friends. … In this inner prayer we can still meditate, but our attention is fixed on the Lord himself.'" –CCC 2709[2]

## Step Four: *Contemplatio*

- Rest in God's presence.

- "Contemplative prayer is also the pre-eminently intense time of prayer. In it the Father strengthens our inner being with power through his Spirit 'that Christ may dwell in [our] hearts through faith' and we may be 'grounded in love.'" –CCC 2714[3]

- "Where does prayer come from? Whether prayer is expressed in words or gestures, it is the whole man who prays. But in naming the source of prayer, Scripture speaks sometimes of the soul or the spirit, but most often of the heart (more than a thousand times). According to Scripture, it is the *heart* that prays. If our heart is far from God, the words of prayer are in vain." –CCC 2562

# DISCUSSION

### QUESTION #1

Was there anything in the teaching this week that surprised you or caused you to rethink your desire to pray with the Scriptures?

### QUESTION #2

Describe your experience of prayer this past week.
Do you feel as if things are getting "easier" as you pray?

### QUESTION #3

Of the four steps of *lectio divina*, which do you think would be the easiest for you to enter into? Which do you think would be the most difficult?

### QUESTION #4

How you feel *lectio divina* can help you as you pray?

### QUESTION #5

Have you made any strides in working through some of your challenges these past few weeks? What challenges still exist?

# DAY 1
WEEK # 3

FOR YOUR PRAYER

# LUKE 12:22-32

Practice the art of *lectio divina*.

JOURNAL

*The "strongest" thought or feeling during my prayer was …*

_____

_____

_____

_____

*My heart "rested" when …*

_____

_____

_____

_____

*I sense the Lord was telling me …*

_____

_____

_____

_____

*I ended the prayer wanting …*

_____

_____

_____

_____

# DAY 2
WEEK # 3

FOR YOUR PRAYER

# PSALM 27

Practice the art of *lectio divina.*

JOURNAL

*The "strongest" thought or feeling during my prayer was …*

_____

_____

_____

_____

*My heart "rested" when …*

_____

_____

_____

_____

*I sense the Lord was telling me …*

_____

_____

_____

_____

*I ended the prayer wanting …*

_____

_____

_____

# DAY 3
WEEK # 3

FOR YOUR PRAYER

# PSALM 23

Practice the art of *lectio divina*.

### JOURNAL

*The "strongest" thought or feeling during my prayer was …*

_____

_____

_____

_____

*My heart "rested" when …*

_____

_____

_____

_____

*I sense the Lord was telling me …*

_____

_____

_____

_____

*I ended the prayer wanting …*

_____

_____

_____

# DAY 4
W E E K   # 3

F O R   Y O U R   P R A Y E R

# JOHN 4:7-19

Practice the art of *lectio divina*.

J O U R N A L

*The "strongest" thought or feeling during my prayer was ...*

_____

_____

_____

_____

*My heart "rested" when ...*

_____

_____

_____

_____

*I sense the Lord was telling me ...*

_____

_____

_____

_____

*I ended the prayer wanting ...*

_____

_____

_____

_____

# DAY 5
### WEEK #3

FOR YOUR PRAYER

# WISDOM 11:21-26

Practice the art of *lectio divina*.

JOURNAL

*The "strongest" thought or feeling during my prayer was …*

_____
_____
_____
_____
_____

*My heart "rested" when …*

_____
_____
_____
_____

*I sense the Lord was telling me …*

_____
_____
_____
_____

*I ended the prayer wanting …*

_____
_____
_____
_____

# DAY 6
WEEK #3

FOR YOUR PRAYER

# DEUTERONOMY 7:6-8

Practice the art of *lectio divina*.

JOURNAL

*The "strongest" thought or feeling during my prayer was …*

_____

_____

_____

_____

*My heart "rested" when …*

_____

_____

_____

_____

*I sense the Lord was telling me …*

_____

_____

_____

_____

*I ended the prayer wanting …*

_____

_____

_____

# DAY 7
### WEEK #3

## FOR YOUR PRAYER

Return to the Scripture passage that spoke to you the most this week.
Practice the art of *lectio divina*.

### JOURNAL

*The "strongest" thought or feeling during my prayer was …*

_____

_____

_____

_____

*My heart "rested" when …*

_____

_____

_____

_____

*I sense the Lord was telling me …*

_____

_____

_____

_____

*I ended the prayer wanting …*

_____

_____

_____

_____

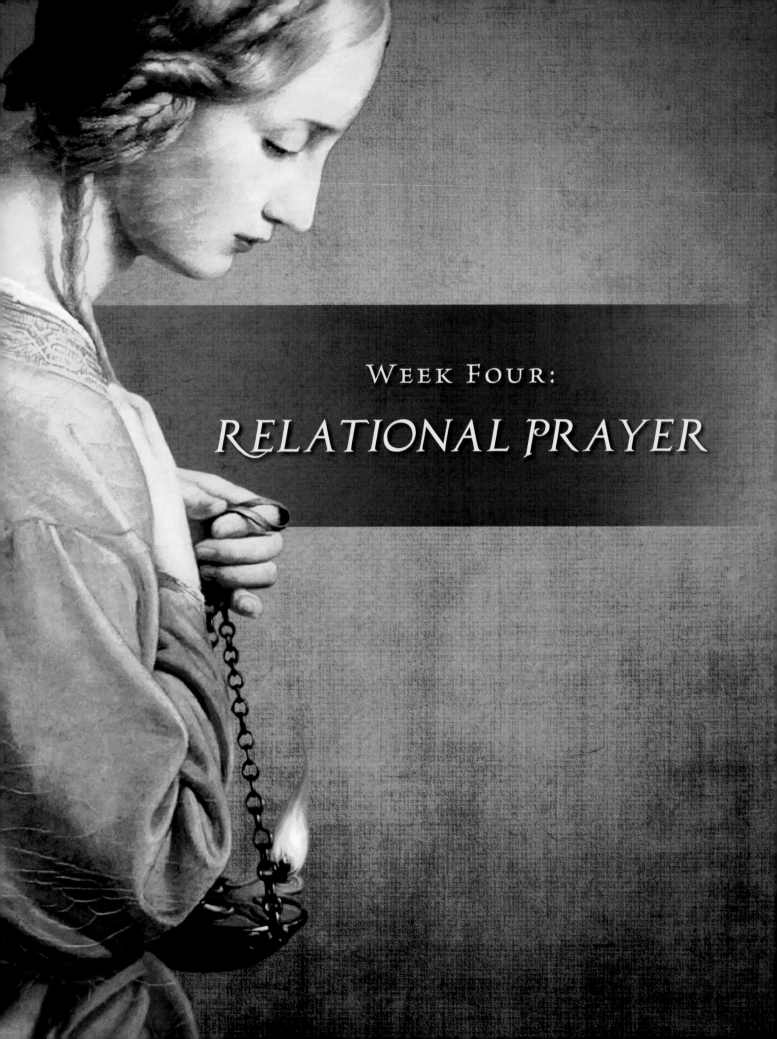

Week Four:

RELATIONAL PRAYER

# Relational Prayer
# SESSION OUTLINE

1. The four steps to relational prayer—prayer in which God reaches out to us, and we respond to his loving approach—may be summed up by the acronym *A.R.R.R.* The four steps are:

   • Acknowledge

   • Relate

   • Receive

   • Respond

2. "Mary is the perfect *Orans* (pray-er), a figure of the Church." –CCC 2679

## Step One: Acknowledge

3. "God calls man first. Man may forget his Creator or hide far from his face; he may run after idols or accuse the deity of having abandoned him; yet the living and true God tirelessly calls each person to that mysterious encounter known as prayer. In prayer … God's initiative of love always comes first; our own first step is always a response." –CCC 2567

## Step Two: Relate

4. "Where does prayer come from? Whether prayer is expressed in words or gestures, it is the whole man who prays. But in naming the source of prayer, Scripture speaks sometimes of the soul or the spirit, but most often of the heart (more than a thousand times). According to Scripture, it is the heart that prays. If our heart is far from God, the words of prayer are in vain." –CCC 2562

5. "In learning how to speak to him, we learn to be a human being, to be ourselves." –Pope Benedict XVI[1]

6. Tips for "Relating" to God.

  • Don't just think about God; talk to God.

  • Be aware. Be honest. Nothing is "off limits."

  • Remember Psalm 139:4 (RSV:CE). "Even before a word is on my tongue, behold, O LORD, you know it altogether."

  • Pay attention to what you do not want to say.

## Step Three: Receive

7. "Always expressed in every prayer … is the truth of the human creature who on the one hand experiences weakness and impoverishment, who therefore addresses his supplication to Heaven, and on the other is endowed with an extraordinary dignity, so that, in preparing to receive the divine Revelation, finds himself able to enter into communion with God." –Pope Benedict XVI[2]

8. "God speaks in silence, but we must know how to listen." –Pope Benedict XVI[3]

9. Tips for "Receiving" from God.

  • Listen. Listen with all your spiritual senses.

  • Be patient. Don't be afraid of the silence.

  • Could be a voice … a song … a memory … an image … a sensation in your body … a Scripture passage.

## Step Four: Respond

10. "The 'yes' of God is not halved, it is not somewhere between 'yes' and 'no,' but is a sound and simple 'yes.' And we respond to this 'yes' with our own 'yes,' with our 'amen,' and so we are sure of the 'yes' of God." –Pope Benedict XVI[4]

11. Tips for "Responding" to God.

  • Respond to what you have received.

  • Could be more conversation … question … laughter … tears … "yes."

  • Together, the four steps of relational prayer (A.R.R.R.) are a vibrant dynamic, not a systematic checklist.

# DISCUSSION

### QUESTION #1

How would you describe your experience in prayer this past week?

### QUESTION #2

Was there anything in the teaching this week that really stands out to you?

### QUESTION #3

We've said that the four steps of relational prayer are:
Acknowledge. Relate. Receive. Respond. (A.R.R.R.)
How could these four distinct steps or movements help you
to relate to God more deeply during prayer?

### QUESTION #4

Which movement within A.R.R.R. is most helpful to you? Which movement is most challenging?

### QUESTION #5

Are you experiencing any obstacles in your prayer?
If so, do you feel like you can be honest with God about those challenges?

# DAY 1
WEEK # 4

FOR YOUR PRAYER

# PSALM 91

Practice the art of *lectio divina*.

Consider how God is the author of all creation.

***Note:*** *Please also read the prayer assignment for tomorrow so that you may adequately prepare.*

JOURNAL

*The "strongest" thought or feeling during my prayer was …*

_____

_____

_____

*My heart "rested" when …*

_____

_____

_____

_____

*I sense the Lord was telling me …*

_____

_____

_____

_____

*I ended the prayer wanting …*

_____

_____

_____

_____

# DAY 2
### WEEK #4

FOR YOUR PRAYER

# GENESIS 1

Watch the sunrise and pray with Genesis 1.

Consider how all of creation is a gift from God, and how all of creation blesses God.

*Note: Please also read the prayer assignment for tomorrow so that you may adequately prepare.*

JOURNAL

*The "strongest" thought or feeling during my prayer was …*

_____

_____

_____

_____

*My heart "rested" when …*

_____

_____

_____

_____

*I sense the Lord was telling me …*

_____

_____

_____

_____

*I ended the prayer wanting …*

_____

_____

_____

_____

# DAY 3
WEEK #4

FOR YOUR PRAYER

# DANIEL 3:35-68

("*The Song of the Three Young Men*" in RSV-CE)

Watch the sunset and pray with Daniel 3:35-68.

Practice the art of *lectio divina.*

Consider how all of creation is a gift from God, and how all of creation blesses God.

JOURNAL

*The "strongest" thought or feeling during my prayer was …*

_____

_____

_____

_____

*My heart "rested" when …*

_____

_____

_____

_____

*I sense the Lord was telling me …*

_____

_____

_____

_____

*I ended the prayer wanting …*

_____

_____

_____

# DAY 4
WEEK #4

FOR YOUR PRAYER

# DANIEL 3:35-68

Again, pray with Daniel 3:35-68.

Practice the art of *lectio divina*.

Consider how all of creation is a gift from God, and how all of creation blesses God.

JOURNAL

*The "strongest" thought or feeling during my prayer was …*

_____

_____

_____

*My heart "rested" when …*

_____

_____

_____

*I sense the Lord was telling me …*

_____

_____

_____

*I ended the prayer wanting …*

_____

_____

_____

# DAY 5
WEEK #4

FOR YOUR PRAYER

# PHILIPPIANS 4:11-13

Practice the art of *lectio divina*.

Ask God for the grace to want him more than you want anything else in this life.

JOURNAL

*The "strongest" thought or feeling during my prayer was …*

_____

_____

_____

*My heart "rested" when …*

_____

_____

_____

*I sense the Lord was telling me …*

_____

_____

_____

*I ended the prayer wanting …*

_____

_____

_____

# DAY 6
WEEK #4

FOR YOUR PRAYER

# PHILIPPIANS 4:11-13

Pray once more with Philippians 4:11-13.

Ask God again for the grace to want him more than you want anything else in this life.

JOURNAL

*The "strongest" thought or feeling during my prayer was …*

_____
_____
_____

*My heart "rested" when …*

_____
_____
_____

*I sense the Lord was telling me …*

_____
_____
_____

*I ended the prayer wanting …*

_____
_____
_____

# DAY 7
WEEK # 4

FOR YOUR PRAYER

Return to the Scripture passage that spoke to you the most this week.
Practice the art of *lectio divina*.
Thank the Lord for all that he has done for you.

JOURNAL

*The "strongest" thought or feeling during my prayer was …*

_____

_____

_____

_____

*My heart "rested" when …*

_____

_____

_____

*I sense the Lord was telling me …*

_____

_____

_____

_____

*I ended the prayer wanting …*

_____

_____

_____

_____

Week Five:

*SPIRITUAL SENSES*

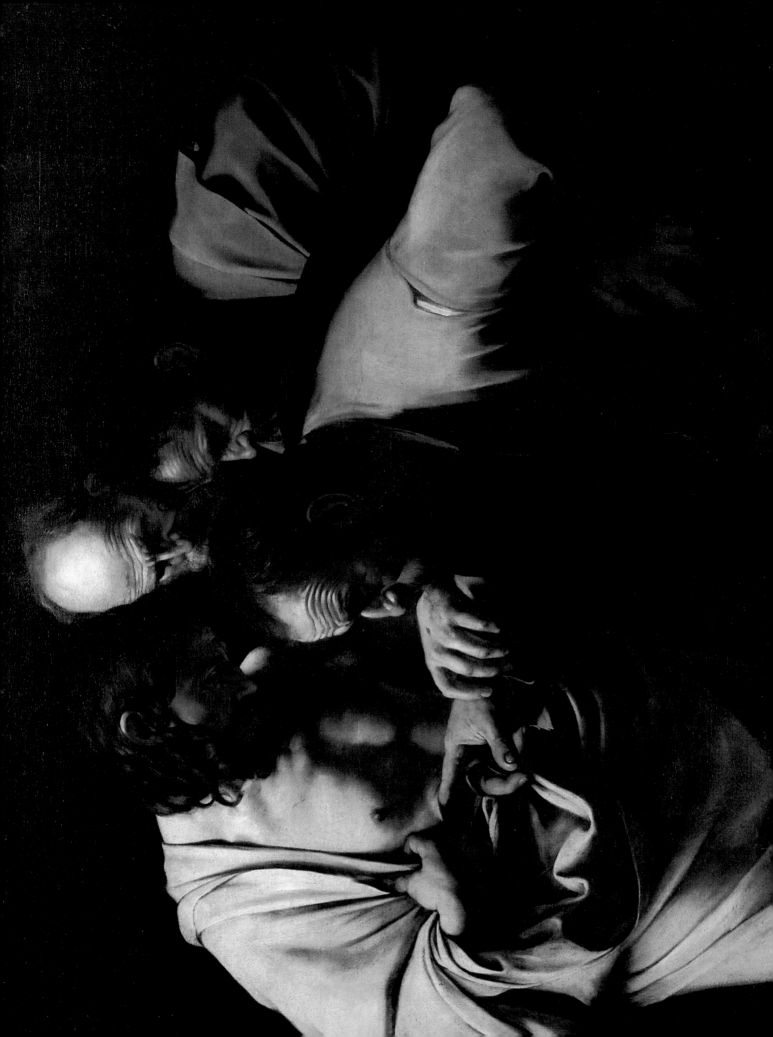

# Spiritual Senses
# SESSION OUTLINE

1. "Meditation engages thought, imagination, emotion, and desire. ... Christian prayer tries above all to meditate on the mysteries of Christ, as in *lectio divina* or the rosary. This form of prayerful reflection is of great value, but Christian prayer should go further: to the knowledge of the love of the Lord Jesus, to union with him." –CCC 2708

2. "Meditation is a prayerful quest engaging thought, imagination, emotion, and desire. Its goal is to make our own in faith the subject considered, by confronting it with the reality of our own life." –CCC 2723

3. Imaginative prayer requires the use of our spiritual senses. Our spiritual senses, used in imaginative prayer, are:

   • Interior sight

   • Interior listening

   • Interior smell

   • Interior feeling

   • Interior tasting

4. "In this manner of praying, Saint Ignatius tells us, we imaginatively see the persons in the Bible passage, we hear the words they speak, and we observe the actions they accomplish in the event." –Fr. Tim Gallagher, O.M.V.[1]

# DISCUSSION

### QUESTION #1

Describe your experience of prayer this past week.

### QUESTION #2

In what ways is your experience of prayer changing? In what ways is it still the same?

### QUESTION #3

How can using your spiritual senses and your imagination help you as you pray?
What challenges, if any, would you anticipate with imaginative prayer?

### QUESTION #4

What stirs in your heart as you gaze at the Caravaggio painting?

### QUESTION #5

If you could be a part of a scene in Jesus' life, which scene would you like to enter? Explain.

# DAY 1
WEEK # 5

# JOHN 20:19-29

Practice the art of imaginative prayer.

Be *in* the scene.

*You* are Thomas ... touch Jesus' wounds.

Let Jesus touch your heart ... and listen.

### JOURNAL

*The "strongest" thought or feeling during my prayer was ...*

_____

_____

_____

*My heart "rested" when ...*

_____

_____

_____

*I sense the Lord was telling me ...*

_____

_____

_____

*I ended the prayer wanting ...*

_____

_____

_____

# DAY 2
WEEK #5

FOR YOUR PRAYER

# JOHN 3:22-30

Practice the art of imaginative prayer.

Be *in* the scene.

Listen to verse 30 ... What is John saying to *you*?

Talk to God about what is on your heart ... and listen.

JOURNAL

*The "strongest" thought or feeling during my prayer was ...*

_____

_____

_____

*My heart "rested" when ...*

_____

_____

_____

*I sense the Lord was telling me ...*

_____

_____

_____

*I ended the prayer wanting ...*

_____

_____

_____

# DAY 3
WEEK #5

FOR YOUR PRAYER

# LUKE 17:11-19

Practice the art of imaginative prayer.

Be *in* the scene.

Listen to verses 17-18 ... Where have *you* been ungrateful?

Talk to God about what is on your heart ... and listen.

JOURNAL

*The "strongest" thought or feeling during my prayer was ...*

_____

_____

_____

*My heart "rested" when ...*

_____

_____

_____

*I sense the Lord was telling me ...*

_____

_____

_____

_____

*I ended the prayer wanting ...*

_____

_____

_____

_____

# DAY 4
WEEK # 5

FOR YOUR PRAYER

# MATTHEW 14:22-33

Practice the art of imaginative prayer.

Be *in* the scene.

*You* are Peter ... *Why* do you take your eyes off of Jesus?

Talk to God about what is on your heart ... and listen.

JOURNAL

*The "strongest" thought or feeling during my prayer was ...*

_____

_____

_____

_____

*My heart "rested" when ...*

_____

_____

_____

*I sense the Lord was telling me ...*

_____

_____

_____

*I ended the prayer wanting ...*

_____

_____

_____

_____

# DAY 5
WEEK # 5

FOR YOUR PRAYER

# MATTHEW 19:16-26

Practice the art of imaginative prayer.

Be *in* the scene.

*You are the rich young man ... Why do you walk away?*

Talk to God about what is on your heart ... and listen.

JOURNAL

*The "strongest" thought or feeling during my prayer was ...*

_____
_____
_____
_____

*My heart "rested" when ...*

_____
_____
_____
_____

*I sense the Lord was telling me ...*

_____
_____
_____
_____

*I ended the prayer wanting ...*

_____
_____
_____
_____

# DAY 6
WEEK # 5

FOR YOUR PRAYER

# JOHN 13:31-38

Practice the art of imaginative prayer.

Be *in* the scene.

*You* are Peter … What stirs in your heart as Jesus makes his prediction?

Talk to God about what is on your heart … and listen.

JOURNAL

*The "strongest" thought or feeling during my prayer was …*

_____

_____

_____

*My heart "rested" when …*

_____

_____

_____

*I sense the Lord was telling me …*

_____

_____

_____

*I ended the prayer wanting …*

_____

_____

_____

# DAY 7
### WEEK # 5

FOR YOUR PRAYER

# JOHN 18:15-18, 25-27

Practice the art of imaginative prayer.

Be *in* the scene.

*You* are Peter ... What stirs in your heart as *you* deny Jesus?

Talk to God about what is on your heart ... and listen.

JOURNAL

*The "strongest" thought or feeling during my prayer was ...*

_____
_____
_____
_____

*My heart "rested" when ...*

_____
_____
_____

*I sense the Lord was telling me ...*

_____
_____
_____

*I ended the prayer wanting ...*

_____
_____
_____

Week Six:

DISCERNMENT
IN PRAYER

# Discernment In Prayer
# SESSION OUTLINE

1.  How do I know it is God who is speaking to me?

2.  "In persons who are going from mortal sin to mortal sin, the enemy is ordinarily accustomed to propose apparent pleasures to them, leading them to imagine sensual delights and pleasures in order to hold them more and make them grow in their vices and sins. In these persons the good spirit uses a contrary method, stinging and biting their consciences through their rational power of moral judgment." –St. Ignatius of Loyola[1]

3.  Going from mortal sin to mortal sin:
    *   Temptation: propose apparent pleasures

    *   Temptation: imagine sensual delights and pleasures

    *   Temptation: hold them more, make them grow in vices and sins

    *   God: stinging and biting the conscience

4.  "In persons who are going on intensely purifying their sins and rising from good to better in the service of God our Lord, the method is contrary to that in the first rule. For then it is proper to the evil spirit to bite, sadden, and place obstacles, disquieting with false reasons, so that the person may not go forward. And it is proper of the good spirit to give courage and strength, consolations, tears, inspirations, and quiet, easing and taking away all obstacles, so that the person may go forward in doing good." –St. Ignatius of Loyola[2]

5. Going on intensely purifying their sins and rising from good to better:

- **Temptation:**
  - bite

  - sadden

  - place obstacles

  - disquieting with false reasons

  - so that the person may not go forward

- **God:**
  - give courage and strength

  - consolations

  - tears

  - inspirations

  - quiet

  - easing and taking away all obstacles

  - so that the person may go forward in doing good

6. "We should give much attention to the course of the thoughts; and if the beginning, middle and end is all good, inclined to all good, it is a sign of the good angel; but if in the course of the thoughts that he brings, it ends in something bad, or distractive, or less good than the soul had proposed to do before, or if it weakens it, or disquiets, or troubles the soul, taking away the peace, tranquility and quiet, which it had before, it is a clear sign that it proceeds from the bad spirit, the enemy of our profit and eternal salvation." –St. Ignatius of Loyola[3]

7. "In those who proceed from good to better, the good angel touches such a soul sweetly, lightly and gently, as a drop of water that enters a sponge; and the bad touches it sharply and with noise and disquiet, as when the drop of water falls on a stone; and in those who proceed from bad to worse the above-said spirits touch in a contrary way; the cause of which is that the disposition of the soul is contrary or similar to the said angels; for when it is contrary, they enter with clamor and sensible disturbances, perceptibly; and when it is similar, they enter with silence, as in their own house through an open door." –St. Ignatius of Loyola[4]

# DISCUSSION

### QUESTION #1

Did you feel the "shift" in the Scripture passages this past week?
How would you describe your experience of prayer this past week?

### QUESTION #2

Did you try using your spiritual senses and imagination in your prayer?
How would you describe your experience?

### QUESTION #3

Was there anything in the teaching this week that surprised you or made you think differently?

### QUESTION #4

Is it difficult for you to discern "what" you hear in prayer?

### QUESTION #5

Notice how tenderly the Good Samaritan is gently cleaning in the Jacopo Bassano painting.
What stirs within you as you gaze at the painting?

# DAY 1
### WEEK # 6

FOR YOUR PRAYER

# PSALM 51

Practice the art of *lectio divina*.

Be *specific* … How have you sinned *specifically*?

Talk to God about what is on your heart … and listen.

After you are finished with your prayer, rewrite Psalm 51 in your own words on the following page.

### JOURNAL

*The "strongest" thought or feeling during my prayer was …*

_____
_____
_____
_____

*My heart "rested" when …*

_____
_____
_____

*I sense the Lord was telling me …*

_____
_____
_____
_____

*I ended the prayer wanting …*

_____
_____
_____

Rewrite Psalm 51 in your own words.

_____

_____

_____

_____

_____

_____

_____

_____

_____

_____

_____

_____

_____

_____

_____

_____

_____

_____

_____

_____

_____

_____

# Day 2
WEEK # 6

FOR YOUR PRAYER

# Psalm 6

Practice the art of *lectio divina*.
Ask God to reveal your sins to you.
Talk to God about what is on your heart … and listen.

JOURNAL

*The "strongest" thought or feeling during my prayer was …*

_____

_____

_____

*My heart "rested" when …*

_____

_____

_____

*I sense the Lord was telling me …*

_____

_____

_____

_____

*I ended the prayer wanting …*

_____

_____

_____

# DAY 3
WEEK # 6

FOR YOUR PRAYER

# LUKE 15:11-16

Practice the art of imaginative prayer.

In the scene, *you* are the son who leaves.

*Why* do you leave? What's your *pattern* of sin?

Talk to God about what is on your heart … and listen.

JOURNAL

*The "strongest" thought or feeling during my prayer was …*

_____

_____

_____

*My heart "rested" when …*

_____

_____

_____

*I sense the Lord was telling me …*

_____

_____

_____

*I ended the prayer wanting …*

_____

_____

_____

# DAY 4
## WEEK # 6

FOR YOUR PRAYER

# ROMANS 7:11-19

Practice the art of *lectio divina*.

Ask God to reveal the root of your sin.

Talk to God about what is on your heart ... and listen.

After you are finished with your prayer, rewrite Romans 7:11-19
in your own words on the following page.

JOURNAL

*The "strongest" thought or feeling during my prayer was ...*

_____

_____

_____

_____

*My heart "rested" when ...*

_____

_____

_____

*I sense the Lord was telling me ...*

_____

_____

_____

*I ended the prayer wanting ...*

_____

_____

_____

Rewrite Romans 7:11-19 in your own words.

_____

_____

_____

_____

_____

_____

_____

_____

_____

_____

_____

_____

_____

_____

_____

_____

_____

_____

_____

_____

_____

_____

_____

# Day 5
WEEK # 6

FOR YOUR PRAYER

# JOHN 8:1-11

Practice the art of imaginative prayer.

In the scene, *you* are the woman caught in adultery.

What is it like for you to raise your head and look at Jesus, *eye to eye*?

Talk to God about what is on your heart.

JOURNAL

*The "strongest" thought or feeling during my prayer was …*

_____
_____
_____
_____

*My heart "rested" when …*

_____
_____
_____

*I sense the Lord was telling me …*

_____
_____
_____
_____

*I ended the prayer wanting …*

_____
_____

# DAY 6
WEEK # 6

FOR YOUR PRAYER

# PSALM 51

Again, pray with this psalm.

Practice the art of *lectio divina*.

Ask God to reveal your sins to you.

Talk to God about what is on your heart ... and listen.

JOURNAL

*The "strongest" thought or feeling during my prayer was ...*

_____

_____

_____

_____

*My heart "rested" when ...*

_____

_____

_____

*I sense the Lord was telling me ...*

_____

_____

_____

_____

*I ended the prayer wanting ...*

_____

_____

_____

# DAY 7
### WEEK # 6

FOR YOUR PRAYER

# PSALM 51

Again, pray with Psalm 51.

Practice the art of *lectio divina*.

Ask God to reveal your sins to you.

Talk to God about what is on your heart ... and listen.

JOURNAL

*The "strongest" thought or feeling during my prayer was ...*

_____

_____

_____

*My heart "rested" when ...*

_____

_____

_____

*I sense the Lord was telling me ...*

_____

_____

_____

*I ended the prayer wanting ...*

_____

_____

_____

Week Seven:

# DEALING WITH DISTRACTIONS

# Dealing With Distractions
# SESSION OUTLINE

1. "In the battle of prayer, we must face in ourselves and around us *erroneous notions of prayer*. Some people view prayer as a simple psychological activity, others as an effort of concentration to reach a mental void. Still others reduce prayer to ritual words and postures. … Those who seek God by prayer are quickly discouraged because they do not know that prayer comes also from the Holy Spirit and not from themselves alone." –CCC 2726

2. "We must also face the fact that certain attitudes deriving from the mentality of 'this present world' can penetrate our lives if we are not vigilant. … Others overly prize production and profit; thus prayer, being unproductive, is useless. … Finally, some see prayer as a flight from the world in reaction against activism; but in fact, Christian prayer is neither an escape from reality nor a divorce from life." –CCC 2727

3. "Prayer is both a gift of grace and a determined response on our part. It always presupposes effort. The great figures of prayer of the Old Covenant before Christ, as well as the Mother of God, the saints, and he himself, all teach us this: prayer is a battle. Against whom? Against ourselves and against the wiles of the tempter who does all he can to turn man away from prayer, away from union with God." –CCC 2725

4. "Finally, our battle has to confront what we experience as *failure in prayer*: discouragement during periods of dryness … disappointment over not being heard according to our own will; wounded pride, stiffened by the indignity that is ours as sinners; our resistance to the idea that prayer is a free and unmerited gift; and so forth. The conclusion is always the same: what good does it do to pray? To overcome these obstacles, we must battle to gain humility, trust, and perseverance." –CCC 2728

5. "The enemy acts like a [spoiled child] in being weak when faced with strength and strong when faced with weakness. For, as it is proper to a [child], when he is fighting with [a firm adult], to lose heart and to flee when the [adult] confronts him firmly, and, on the contrary, if the [adult] begins to flee, losing heart, the anger, vengeance and ferocity of the [child] grow greatly and know no bounds, in the same way, it is proper to the enemy to weaken and lose heart, fleeing and ceasing his temptations when the person who is exercising himself in spiritual things confronts the temptations of the enemy firmly, doing what is diametrically opposed to them; and, on the contrary, if the person who is exercising himself begins to be afraid and lose heart in suffering the temptations, there is no beast so fierce on the face of the earth as the enemy of human nature in following out his damnable intention with such growing malice." –St. Ignatius of Loyola[1]

# DISCUSSION

### QUESTION #1

Describe your experience of prayer this past week.

### QUESTION #2

How would describe our culture's opinion of sin?
How would describe your opinion of sin?

### QUESTION #3

Gaze at Rembrandt's painting of the Prodigal Son. What stirs within you?

### QUESTION #4

What is your experience of distractions?
What are some of the more common distractions you experience?
How do you generally deal with distractions?

### QUESTION #5

What interested you most during this week's teaching?

# DAY 1
### WEEK #7

# LUKE 15:11-24

Practice the art of imaginative prayer.

In the scene, *you* are the prodigal son.

Focus on the Father's eyes in verse 20.

Notice the Father's compassion.

What is the Father saying to you in his eyes?

### JOURNAL

*The "strongest" thought or feeling during my prayer was …*

_____

_____

_____

_____

*My heart "rested" when …*

_____

_____

_____

_____

*I sense the Lord was telling me …*

_____

_____

_____

_____

_____

*I ended the prayer wanting …*

_____

_____

_____

_____

# DAY 2
### WEEK #7

FOR YOUR PRAYER

# LUKE 7:36-50

Practice the art of imaginative prayer.

In the scene, you are at Jesus' feet … focus on verse 48.

Look *at* Jesus. What is Jesus saying *to you* in his eyes?

Talk to God about what is on your heart … and listen.

JOURNAL

*The "strongest" thought or feeling during my prayer was …*

_____

_____

_____

_____

*My heart "rested" when …*

_____

_____

_____

_____

*I sense the Lord was telling me …*

_____

_____

_____

_____

*I ended the prayer wanting …*

_____

_____

_____

_____

# DAY 3
WEEK #7

FOR YOUR PRAYER

# EZEKIEL 36:23-29

Practice the art of *lectio divina*.

Talk to God about what is on your heart … and listen.

Make a commitment to go to a Catholic priest to receive the sacrament of reconciliation this week.*

JOURNAL

*The "strongest" thought or feeling during my prayer was …*

_____

_____

_____

_____

*My heart "rested" when …*

_____

_____

_____

*I sense the Lord was telling me …*

_____

_____

_____

*I ended the prayer wanting …*

_____

_____

_____

*Most parishes offer confessions on Saturdays, but if you have scheduling difficulties many parishes are willing to schedule a specific time for you if you call in advance.

# DAY 4
WEEK #7

FOR YOUR PRAYER

# 1 PETER 2:21-25

Pray with 1 Peter 2:21-25.

Thank Jesus for his sacrifice, for the Church he founded, and for the sacrament of reconciliation.

JOURNAL

*The "strongest" thought or feeling during my prayer was …*

_____

_____

_____

*My heart "rested" when …*

_____

_____

_____

*I sense the Lord was telling me …*

_____

_____

_____

*I ended the prayer wanting …*

_____

_____

_____

# DAY 5
WEEK #7

FOR YOUR PRAYER

# PSALM 118

Practice the art of *lectio divina*.

Considering the past few days … the past few weeks, what are you most thankful for?

Talk to God about what is on your heart.

After you are finished with your prayer, rewrite Psalm 118 in your own words on the following page.

JOURNAL

*The "strongest" thought or feeling during my prayer was …*

_____

_____

_____

_____

*My heart "rested" when …*

_____

_____

_____

_____

*I sense the Lord was telling me …*

_____

_____

_____

_____

*I ended the prayer wanting …*

_____

_____

_____

Rewrite Psalm 118 in your own words.

_____

_____

_____

_____

_____

_____

_____

_____

_____

_____

_____

_____

_____

_____

_____

_____

_____

_____

_____

_____

_____

_____

_____

_____

_____

# DAY 6
WEEK #7

FOR YOUR PRAYER

# JOHN 21:15-19

Practice the art of imaginative prayer

In the scene, you are Peter ... Do *you* love *Jesus*?

Would you do anything *for him*?

Would you follow *the Lord* anywhere?

Talk to God about what is on your heart.

JOURNAL

*The "strongest" thought or feeling during my prayer was ...*

_____

_____

_____

_____

*My heart "rested" when ...*

_____

_____

_____

_____

*I sense the Lord was telling me ...*

_____

_____

_____

_____

*I ended the prayer wanting ...*

_____

_____

_____

# DAY 7
WEEK #7

FOR YOUR PRAYER

Reread your journal from weeks five through six

Considering the past few days … the past few weeks, what are you most thankful for?

What has God done for you?

Celebrate with Jesus and talk with Him … and listen.

JOURNAL

*The "strongest" thought or feeling during my prayer was …*

_____

_____

_____

_____

*My heart "rested" when …*

_____

_____

_____

_____

*I sense the Lord was telling me …*

_____

_____

_____

_____

*I ended the prayer wanting …*

_____

_____

_____

_____

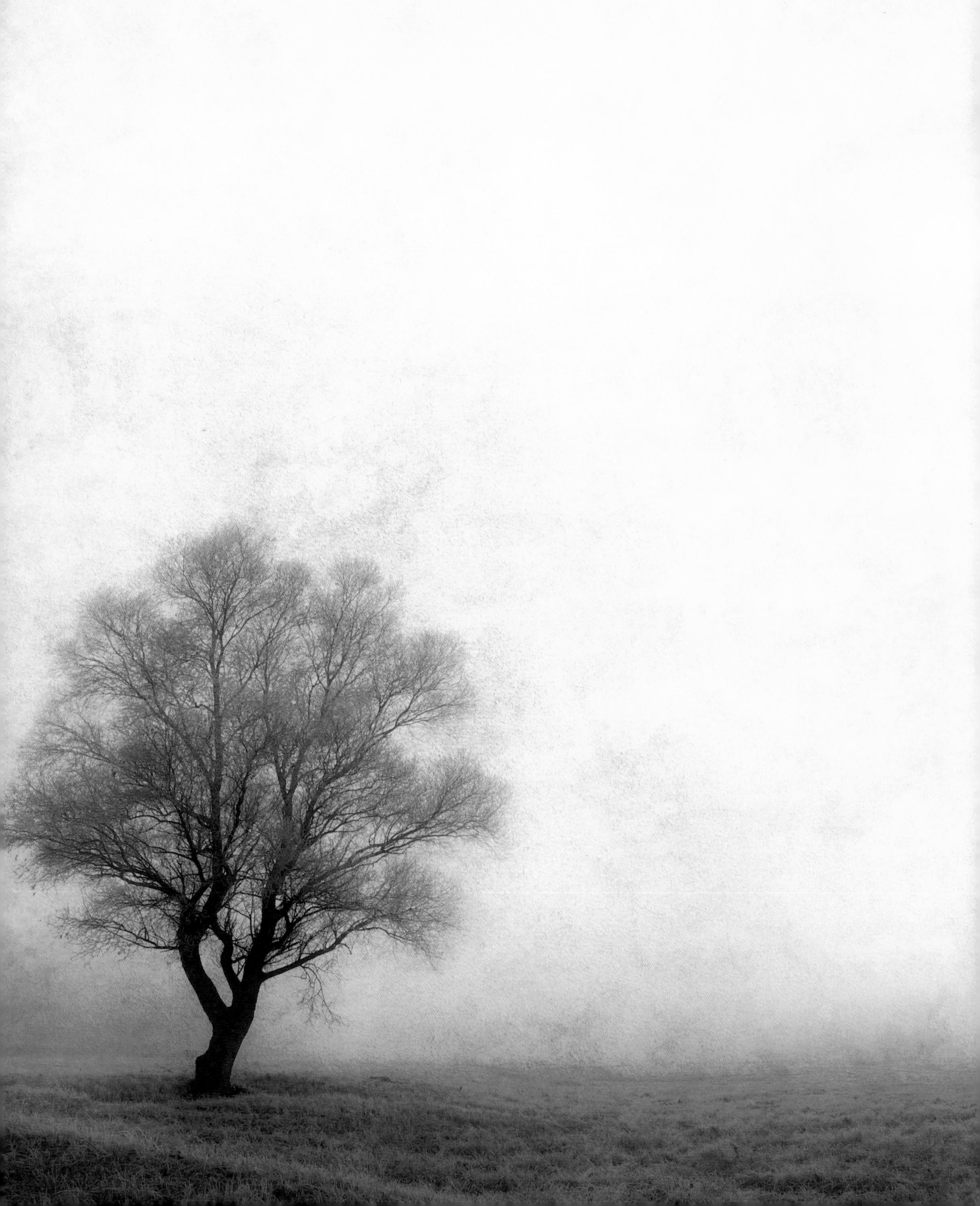

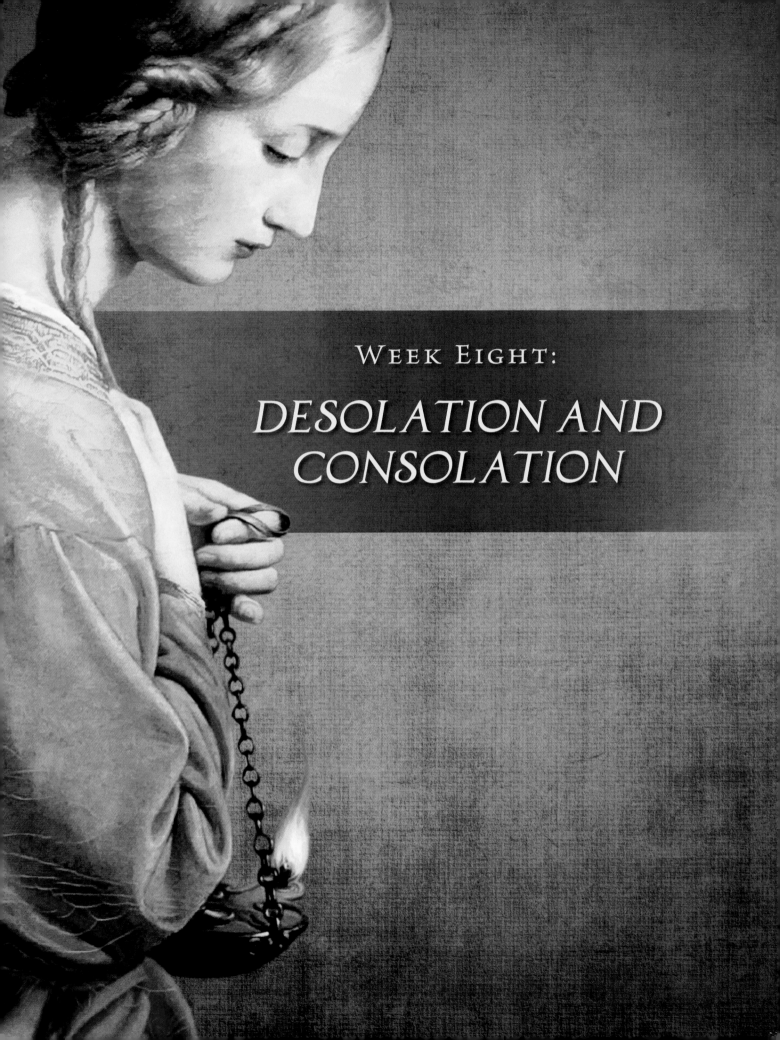

Week Eight:

# DESOLATION AND CONSOLATION

## Desolation and Consolation
# SESSION OUTLINE

1.  "Another difficulty, especially for those who sincerely want to pray, is *dryness*. Dryness belongs to contemplative prayer when the heart is separated from God, with no taste for thoughts, memories, and feelings, even spiritual ones. ... If dryness is due to the lack of roots, because the word has fallen on rocky soil, the battle requires conversion." –CCC 2731

2.  "Finally, our battle has to confront what we experience as failure in prayer: discouragement during periods of dryness ... disappointment over not being heard according to our own will; wounded pride, stiffened by the indignity that is ours as sinners; our resistance to the idea that prayer is a free and unmerited gift; and so forth. The conclusion is always the same: what good does it do to pray? To overcome these obstacles, we must battle to gain humility, trust, and perseverance." –CCC 2728

3.  "I call desolation ... darkness of soul, disturbance in it, movement to low and earthly things, disquiet from various agitations and temptations, moving to lack of confidence, without hope, without love, finding oneself totally slothful, tepid, sad, and as if separated from one's Creator and Lord. For just as consolation is contrary to desolation,* in the same way the thoughts that come from consolation are contrary to the thoughts that come from desolation." –St. Ignatius of Loyola[1]

*"There are three principal causes for which we find ourselves desolate. The first is because we are tepid, slothful or negligent in our spiritual exercises, and so through our faults spiritual consolation withdraws from us. The second, to try us and see how much we are and how much we extend ourselves in his service and praise without so much payment of consolations and increased graces. The third, to give us true recognition and understanding so that we may interiorly feel that it is not ours to attain or maintain increased devotion, intense love, tears or any other spiritual consolation, but that all is the gift and grace of God our Lord, and so that we may not build a nest in something belonging to another, raising our mind in some pride or vainglory, attributing to ourselves the devotion or the other parts of the spiritual consolation." St. Ignatius of Loyola[2]

4. "Let one who is in desolation work to be in patience, which is contrary to the vexations which come to him, and let him think that he will soon be consoled, diligently using the means against such desolation, as is said in the sixth rule." –St. Ignatius of Loyola[3]

5. "We can find fresh courage for accepting with patience and faith every situation of difficulty, affliction and trial in the knowledge that from the darkness the Lord will cause a new day to dawn." –Pope Benedict XVI[4]

6. "Dear brothers and sisters, God's way of acting—very different from ours—gives us comfort, strength and hope because God does not withdraw his 'yes.' In the face of stressful human relations, even in the family, we often fail to persevere in freely given love which demands commitment and sacrifice. Instead, God does not grow tired of us; he never wearies of being patient with us and, with his immense mercy, always leads the way and reaches out to us first: his 'yes' is absolutely reliable." –Pope Benedict XVI[5]

# DISCUSSION

### QUESTION #1

Describe your experience of prayer this past week.

### QUESTION #2

What do you connect with as you read Saint Ignatius' description of desolation?

### QUESTION #3

What do you normally do in times of desolation?
Do you feel like God is still with you during these times? Explain.

### QUESTION #4

How have you grown during the past eight weeks? What have you learned through *Oremus?*

### QUESTION #5

What can you do so that you continue to grow?

# DAY 1
WEEK #8

## FOR YOUR PRAYER

# LUKE 2:1-14

Practice the art of imaginative prayer.
In the scene, *you* are near the manger *with* Mary as she gives birth to Jesus.
Talk to God about what is on your heart ... and listen.

### J O U R N A L

*The "strongest" thought or feeling during my prayer was ...*

_____
_____
_____
_____

*My heart "rested" when ...*

_____
_____
_____
_____

*I sense the Lord was telling me ...*

_____
_____
_____
_____

*I ended the prayer wanting ...*

_____
_____
_____

#  DAY 2
WEEK #8

FOR YOUR PRAYER

# LUKE 2:21-38

Practice the art of imaginative prayer.

In the scene, *you* are with Mary and Joseph as they present Jesus in the Temple.

Talk to God about what is on your heart ... and listen.

JOURNAL

*The "strongest" thought or feeling during my prayer was ...*

_____

_____

_____

_____

*My heart "rested" when ...*

_____

_____

_____

_____

*I sense the Lord was telling me ...*

_____

_____

_____

_____

*I ended the prayer wanting ...*

_____

_____

_____

_____

# DAY 3
### WEEK #8

FOR YOUR PRAYER

# LUKE 2:41-50

Practice the art of imaginative prayer.
In the scene, you are with Mary and Joseph as they search for Jesus.
Talk to God about what is on your heart … and listen.

### JOURNAL

*The "strongest" thought or feeling during my prayer was …*

_____
_____
_____
_____

*My heart "rested" when …*

_____
_____
_____
_____

*I sense the Lord was telling me …*

_____
_____
_____
_____

*I ended the prayer wanting …*

_____
_____
_____
_____

# DAY 4
WEEK # 8

FOR YOUR PRAYER

# LUKE 2:51-52

Practice the art of imaginative prayer.
In the scene, you are with Mary and Joseph in Nazareth.
Be with Jesus as he grows in age.
Ask them to show you the hidden years of Jesus' life.
Talk to God about what is on your heart.

JOURNAL

*The "strongest" thought or feeling during my prayer was …*

_____

_____

_____

*My heart "rested" when …*

_____

_____

_____

*I sense the Lord was telling me …*

_____

_____

_____

*I ended the prayer wanting …*

_____

_____

_____

# DAY 5
#### WEEK # 8

FOR YOUR PRAYER

# MATTHEW 3:13-17

Practice the art of imaginative prayer.

In the scene, *you* are Jesus in line in the river.

Listen as the Father pronounces Jesus as his beloved Son.

Ask the Father to speak those same words to *you*.

Talk to God about what is on your heart.

### JOURNAL

*The "strongest" thought or feeling during my prayer was ...*

_____
_____
_____
_____

*My heart "rested" when ...*

_____
_____
_____
_____

*I sense the Lord was telling me ...*

_____
_____
_____
_____

*I ended the prayer wanting ...*

_____
_____
_____
_____

# Day 6
### WEEK # 8

FOR YOUR PRAYER

# JOHN 1:35-39

Practice the art of imaginative prayer.

In the scene, *you* are with John the Baptist.

Go to Jesus in verse 37.

"Where" does he take you in verse 39?

Talk to God about what is on your heart.

JOURNAL

*The "strongest" thought or feeling during my prayer was …*

_____
_____
_____

*My heart "rested" when …*

_____
_____
_____

*I sense the Lord was telling me …*

_____
_____
_____

*I ended the prayer wanting …*

_____
_____
_____

# DAY 7
### WEEK #8

FOR YOUR PRAYER

# MATTHEW 4:18-21

Practice the art of imaginative prayer.

In the scene, *you* are Peter.

Jesus looks you in the eyes and asks you to follow him.

What do you say?

Talk to God about what is on your heart.

JOURNAL

*The "strongest" thought or feeling during my prayer was …*

_____

_____

_____

*My heart "rested" when …*

_____

_____

_____

*I sense the Lord was telling me …*

_____

_____

_____

*I ended the prayer wanting …*

_____

_____

_____

# Some Final Thoughts from Fr. Mark Toups

"Now what? Where do we go from here?"

Perhaps you have heard those questions. Perhaps you have asked those questions. These questions echoed within the disciples in Luke, chapter 24.

Grieving Jesus' death, and worried about their future, the disciples walked "to a village named Emmaus, about seven miles from Jerusalem," (Luke 24:13). The risen Christ entered into the anxiety as he meets them along the way. While "their eyes were kept from recognizing him," their hearts "burned within" while he talked with them (see Luke 24:16, 32).

During the last eight weeks, we have shared a sacred pilgrimage. Perhaps you know the hearts of the Emmaus disciples, for perhaps you too have had your heart "burning" within. You have learned how to pray in new ways. You have grown in intimacy with Jesus, our Bridegroom. You have received direction in your spiritual life.

Now what? Where do we go from here?

*Return.* Saint Ignatius of Loyola would invite you to return to the moments on this journey when you have experienced God's presence the most. What meditations spoke most to you? What words enflamed your heart? What did Jesus say to you? The moments of grace that you experienced then might still be pregnant with grace for you to experience now. Returning to those meditations helps you "unpack" further what God has in store for you.

*Reread your journal.* Make a list of the meditations or prayer experiences that were most efficacious. Once you have your list, take time to "revisit" them one at a time. Perhaps you will spend more than one day "lingering" in the grace of a particular meditation. If so, stay there … "sit" in the meditation for another day … or a week … or longer. Once the well has run dry on that particular mediation, move on to the next one that made an impact on you.

*Resources.* There are a few resources that may be helpful for you as you continue.

**For more on praying with the Scriptures:**

- *Praying Scripture for a Change: An Introduction to Lectio Divina,* by Tim Gray (Ascension Press)

- *Walking with God: A Journey Through the Bible* by Tim Gray and Jeff Cavins (Ascension Press)

- *WRAP Yourself in Scripture,* by Karen and Lawrence Dwyer (IPF Publishing), is a concise, yet packed, introduction to *lectio divina.* It is a great resource to help you deepen your experience of praying with the Scriptures.

**For more on prayer and growth in holiness:**

- *Communion with Christ* by Deacon James Keating (IPF Publishing)

- *Listening for Truth: Praying Our Way to Virtue* by Deacon James Keating (Liguori). This is a beautifully written invitation to grow further in the spiritual life. Essentially, once we have grown in intimacy with Christ, we should soon grow in our life of virtue. As the old spiritual sings, "Something on the inside, working on the outside, O' what change in my life!" Celebrate the "change in your life" and grow in virtue.

- *A School of Prayer* by Pope Benedict XVI (Scepter Publishers)

**For more on consolation, desolation, and discerning little things:**

- *The Discernment of Spirits: An Ignatian Guide for Everyday Living,* by Timothy Gallagher, O.M.V. (Crossroad) is an easy-to-read teaching on Saint Ignatius of Loyola's Rules for the Discernment of Spirits. Saint Ignatius reminds us that desolation and consolation are expected in the spiritual life. Everyone experiences desolation and consolation. The wisdom of Saint Ignatius teaches us how to respond to desolation and how to receive the fullness of consolation.

- *The Examine Prayer: Ignatian Wisdom for Our Lives Today,* by Tim Gallagher, O.M.V. (Crossroad)

**Classics on the spiritual life:**

- *Abandonment to Divine Providence* by Jean-Pierre de Caussade

- *The Imitation of Christ* by Thomas a Kempis

- *An Introduction to the Devout Life* by St. Francis de Sales

- *The Three Conversions in the Spiritual Life* by Reginald Garrigou-Lagrange

**To learn more about Blessed John Paul II's Theology of the Body:**

- *Theology of the Body for Beginners* (Ascension Press)

- *Man & Woman He Created Them: A Theology of the Body* (Pauline Books and Media)

Finally, trust that God is pursuing you. God wants you and will "tirelessly" call you to "that mysterious encounter known as prayer" (CCC 2567). The pressure is not on you. The pressure is on God. Let the Lord call you, and expect amazing things to happen.

The most important thing is to show up. Keep showing up. Stay faithful to your commitment to pray, and trust that God will do the rest.

Receive the gift of prayer.

It has been a pleasure serving you. Let's keep praying for each other.

# Endnotes

### A Letter from Fr. Toups
1. Pope Benedict XVI, Address of his Holiness Benedict XVI to the participants in the International Congress Organized to Commemorate the 40th Anniversary of the Dogmatic Constitution on Divine Revelation "Dei Verbum." Sept. 16, 2005.
2. Hans Urs von Balthazar, *Prayer* (San Francisco: Ignatius Press, 1986), 7.
3. *Prayer,* 7.
4. St. Therese of Lisieux, *Manuscrips autobiographiques,* C 25r.

### Week One: What is Prayer?
1. Cf. *Acts* 17:27.
2. Pope Benedict XVI, General Audience, May 4, 2011
3. Hans Urs von Balthazar, *Prayer* (San Francisco: Ignatius Press, 1986), 7.
4. Pope Benedict XVI, General Audience, May 4, 2011, quoting Luke 11:1.
5. St. Ignatius of Loyola, *Spiritual Exercises #75.*
6. Pope Benedict XVI, *Deus Caritas Est,* 1.
7. Pope Benedict XVI, General Audience, May 4, 2011.
8. Pope Benedict XVI, General Audience, May 11, 2011.

### Week Two: Before You Pray
1. Pope Benedict XVI, General Audience, August 3, 2011.
2. Pope Benedict XVI, General Audience, August 17, 2011.
3. Pope Benedict XVI, *Spe Salvi #33*
4. Pope Benedict XVI, General Audience, May 25, 2011
5. Pope Benedict XVI, General Audience, May 23, 2012
6. Saint Ignatius of Loyola, *Spiritual Exercises #48*

### Week Three: *Lectio Divina*
1. Pope Benedict XVI, Congress of Biblical Scholars, Rome, September 2005.
2. St. Teresa of Jesus, *The Book of Her Life,* 8, 5, in *The Collected Works of St. Teresa of Avila.* Tr. K.Kavanaugh, O.C.D., and O. Rodriguez, O.C.D. (Washington DC: Institute of Carmelite Studies, 1976), I, 67.
3. *Eph.* 3:16-17.

### Week Four: Relational Prayer
1. Pope Benedict XVI, General Audience, June 22, 2011.
2. Pope Benedict XVI, General Audience, May 4, 2011.
3. Pope Benedict XVI, General Audience, August 10, 2011.
4. Pope Benedict XVI, General Audience, May 30, 2012.

**Week Five: Spiritual Senses**
1. Fr. Tim Gallagher, O.M.V., *Meditation and Contemplation* (New York: Crossroad Publishing Company, 2008), 36.

**Week Six: Discernment in Prayer**
1. Saint Ignatius of Loyola, *Spiritual Exercises #314*, as translated by Timothy M. Gallagher, O.M.V., in *The Discernment of Spirits* (New York: Crossroads Publishing, 2011), 7).
2. Saint Ignatius of Loyola, *Spiritual Exercises #315*, in *Discernment of Spirits*, 7.
3. Saint Ignatius of Loyola, *Spiritual Exercises #333*, in *Discernment of Spirits*.
4. Saint Ignatius of Loyola, *Spiritual Exercises #335*, in *Discernment of Spirits*, 41.

**Week Seven: Dealing With Distractions**
1. St. Ignatius of Loyola, *Spiritual Exercises #325*.

**Week Eight: Desolation and Consolation**
1. Saint Ignatius of Loyola, *Spiritual Exercises #316*, in *Discernment of Spirits*, 8.
2. Saint Ignatius of Loyola, *Spiritual Exercises #322*, in *Discernment of Spirits*, 9.
3. Saint Ignatius of Loyola, *Spiritual Exercises #321*, in *Discernment of Spirits*, 8.
4. Pope Benedict XVI, General Audience, February 22, 2012.
5. Pope Benedict XVI, General Audience, May 30, 2012.

# Artwork

**Week One,** *The Annunciation,* by Henry Ossawa Tanner (1859-1937)

**Week Two,** *Creation of Adam,* by Michelangelo Buonarroti (1475-1564)

**Week Three,** *Song of the Angels,* by William-Adolphe Bouguereau (1825-1905)

**Week Four,** *Christ in the Carpenter's Shop,* by Georges de La Tour (1593-1652)

**Week Five,** *The Doubting of St. Thomas,* by Michelangelo Merisi Caravaggio (1571-1610)

**Week Six,** *The Good Samaritan,* by Jacopo Bassano (1510 - 1592)

**Week Seven,** *The Return of the Prodigal Son,* by Rembrandt Harmensz van Rijn (1606–1669)

**Week Eight,** *The Descent of the Holy Spirit,* by Anthony van Dyck (1599–1641)

# Acknowledgments

I am deeply grateful to the many people whose assistance made *Oremus* possible:

I would like to thank those who taught me how to pray, namely: Rev. John Horn, SJ, president-Rector of Kenrick-Glennon Seminary in St. Louis, Missouri; Kathleen Kanavy, Director of Spiritual Director Formation for the Institute for Priestly Formation; and Rev. F. Hampton Davis III, Diocese of Lafayette. Much of *Oremus* comes from my personal experience of prayer, and I am indebted to those who were patient with me.

I would like to thank the Institute for Priestly Formation. The mission of IPF is to help priests fall in love and stay in love so that love for God determines everything in their life. God saved my life through the ministry of IPF. Furthermore, IPF taught me everything that is *Oremus*. Without IPF, *Oremus* would not be. Without IPF, my priesthood might not be. Thank you, IPF, for teaching me, forming me, and loving me. Specifically, I would like to acknowledge IPF for their articulation of "ARRR: Acknowledge, Relate, Receive, Respond." Thank you for granting permission in allowing me to share your gift of prayer.

I would like to thank Mr. Brian Butler, founder and president of Dumb Ox Productions, and Mr. Roch Gernon, also with Dumb Ox Productions, for their vision. Without them *Oremus* most likely would have remained a small project within the homes of south Louisiana. Thank you for your brotherhood and vision.

I would like to thank Matt Pinto and everyone at Ascension Press, including Steve Motyl, Patrick McCabe, Chris Cope, Heidi Saxton, Mike Fontecchio, and Stella Ziegler. Without the trust and vision of Ascension Press, *Oremus* would not be. Thank you for remaining a leader in the New Evangelization. Thank you for committing to bring the Gospel to a searching generation. In addition, I would like to thank Philip Braun for his holiness, vision, and productive expertise.

I would like to thank the Most Rev. Sam G. Jacobs, Bishop of the Diocese of Houma-Thibodaux, for his spiritual fatherhood and for encouraging me to pursue writing. I would also like to thank the Most Rev. Gregory M. Aymond, Archbishop of New Orleans, for his shepherding me when I was a seminarian, as well as for his assistance with filming within the Archdiocese of New Orleans.

I would like to thank the beautiful parishioners of St. Lucy's Catholic Church in Houma, Louisiana and St. Luke's Catholic Church in Thibodaux, Louisiana. You lured *Oremus* from my heart. It was my gift to you and now your gift is blessing others. I will always remember you with great affection.

Finally, and most importantly, I would like to thank God, the Father, "from whom every family in heaven and on earth is named" (Eph: 3:15, NAB). Thank you for your mercy, your fidelity, and your gaze. I pray that the same Father "may grant you in accord with the riches of his glory to be strengthened with power through his Spirit in the inner self and that Christ may dwell in your hearts through faith; that you, rooted and grounded in love, may have strength to comprehend with all the holy ones what is the breadth and length and height and depth, and to know the love of Christ that surpasses knowledge, so that you may be filled with all the fullness of God. Now to him who is able to accomplish far more than all we ask or imagine, by the power at work within us to him be glory in the church and in Christ Jesus to all generations, forever and ever. Amen," (Eph 3:16-21, NAB).